Crackbones
Saves
the School

Alan MacDonald

Illustrated by Doffy Weir

OXFORD
UNIVERSITY PRESS

It was the first day of term at Abbey Park School. Class 4 sat in neat rows. They sat up straight. Nobody talked or picked their nose. The Head, Miss Lupin, had told them to wait quietly for their new teacher.

Suddenly the door flew open.
The new teacher strode in.
He had a black patch over
one eye and a sword at his
belt. His beard hung in thick
dark curls.

'Ahoy, mates! The name's
Blackbones, Captain Blackbones!'
he bellowed.

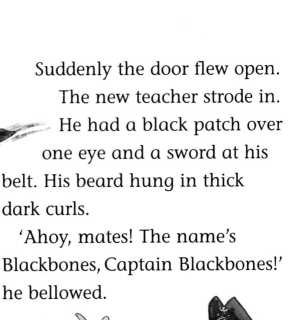

Blackbones sat down on top of
his desk. He kicked off his black
boots, showing a hole in one sock.

Class 4 gasped as he pulled out his sword – and used it to sharpen a pencil.

He pointed at Yasmin.

'You, matey, what lesson is it?'

'Please Captain, geography.'

Blackbones stroked his beard.

'Ge-og-ruffy. Never heard of it. We'll start with Art.'

Lessons began. They painted a skull and crossbones on the classroom door. With their rulers, they practised sword fighting.

Blackbones winked. 'Now you looks like proper pirates. Let's sail for the sea.'

'The sea's miles away,' said Adrian.

'And Miss Lupin doesn't let us go on trips,' said Yasmin.

Tara had an idea.

'What about the school swimming pool?'

'Just the job! Set sail for the swimming pool!' roared Blackbones. He was enjoying himself. Teaching was far more fun than he'd expected.

Miss Lupin was in the swimming pool with Class 3 when the door burst open.

'Captain Blackbones…!' she began.
But it was too late. Blackbones ordered
his pirates forward. 'Enemy ahoy!'

Miss Lupin watched in horror as the
pirates of Class 4 charged past her.
They didn't even stop to change into
their swimsuits. They jumped straight
into the pool yelling, 'Yo ho ho!'

Class 3 threw rubber rings at the
pirates. The pirates threw back plastic
floats. Blackbones was everywhere,
waving his sword and shouting orders.
It was just like the good old days.

All of a sudden Miss Lupin's whistle
split the air. Most of Class 3 were up on
the diving board. The pirates were
about to make them walk the plank.

Blackbones pointed to his class.
'Rattle me cutlass, Miss Lupin. Did I
teach 'em well or not?'

Miss Lupin turned to him with a face as black as thunder.

'Get those children down this minute!' she ordered. 'And you, Captain, I want to see you in my office right away.'

Blackbones spent all afternoon in Miss Lupin's office. When he came back he threw his hat on the floor.

'Barnacles!' he muttered.

11

Tara and Yasmin had waited behind to see him. 'What happened? What did Miss Lupin say?' they asked.

'I've got to go, shipmates,' said Blackbones sadly.

'You mean Miss Lupin has sacked you? After only one day?'

The girls couldn't believe it.

Blackbones sighed. 'I guess I'm no use as a teacher.'

'You're the best teacher we've ever had,' said Yasmin.

Blackbones put on his hat.

'Kind of you to say so, maties. But I've got to go by the end of the week, right after the school fair.'

Tara and Yasmin walked away sadly. If only they hadn't fought Class 3 in the swimming pool. Now Blackbones was going. And they would never get a teacher like him again.

As they passed Miss Lupin's office they heard voices inside. 'We need £10,000 – and that's just to mend the roof!' sighed Miss Lupin.

'This school was started by my Great Aunt Amelia. It's been here two hundred years. Now I'll have to close it down.'

'Maybe the school fair will go well this year?' said Miss Punter, the games teacher.

Miss Lupin shook her head. 'It will take a miracle to make £10,000.'

The two girls were listening outside. Tara grabbed Yasmin's arm. 'That's it!' she said. 'That's how we'll save the captain!'

Next day Tara explained her idea to the rest of Class 4.

All they needed was a way to make £10,000 at the school fair. The school would be saved. And Miss Lupin would be so pleased, she would give Blackbones back his job.

'We could sell cakes.
I can make them in cookery,'
said Fiona.

'Your cakes are like lumps of
rock,' said Mungo.

'Let's kidnap Miss Lupin.
We could demand £10,000 to
set her free,' said Adrian.

But no one could see anyone
paying 10p for Miss Lupin, let alone
£10,000.

Blackbones looked up. He was
mending the hole in his sock.

'Tea and cakes are for old folk,' he
said. 'Give me the sea breeze in my
hair and a treasure map in my hand.
That's the life for a pirate.'

Tara jumped up and clapped
her hands.

'That's it! A treasure hunt. Great
idea, Captain!'

'But we haven't got any treasure,'
Yasmin said.

'We don't need any. We'll just sell
lots of maps. Each map will show
the treasure in a different place.
That'll keep people digging all day,'
said Tara.

The day of the school fair arrived. Miss Lupin greeted the crowds. She hoped they would spend lots of money.

'But we'll never make £10,000,' she sighed. 'I'll have to close the old school down. What would Great Aunt Amelia say?'

She passed the stall run by Class 4.

Captain Blackbones was standing on a box. 'Find the buried treasure!' he was shouting. 'Have a go, matey! Buy a map and dig for pirate gold!'

'What a good idea!' said an old lady. 'You look just like a real pirate.'

Adrian and Yasmin were selling treasure maps. On every map was a skull and crossbones. An X marked where the treasure was. Blackbones had drawn the maps himself and they were selling like hot cakes.

'I thought I told you to forget about pirates,' said Miss Lupin crossly.

'It's a pirate treasure hunt,' said
Tara. 'It was the Captain's idea.'

Miss Lupin glared at Blackbones.

'Buried treasure! Stuff and nonsense!
The sooner you're out of this school the
better.'

But the treasure hunt was the
star of the fair. Everywhere Miss
Lupin went she saw people
puzzling over treasure maps.
It was only later that they
began digging.

Mr Bliss, the music teacher, came running up. 'Miss Lupin… it's the games field,' he panted. 'Come and look.'

Miss Lupin went with him. The games field had gone. In every corner people were digging for buried treasure.

It was the same story on the front lawn. Dads with pick axes had started on the car park. Some were even taking up the floor in the school hall.

Miss Lupin sat down on the grass. She felt ill. Her school looked as if it had been bombed.

'Excuse me,' said a man with a spade. 'Would you mind moving? I want to dig for treasure there.'

Miss Lupin went to look for Blackbones.

She found him counting out money.

'Rattle me cutlass! We made over £100!'

He showed her the money. But Miss Lupin's face had gone purple.

'Look what you've done to my school! It's ruined! Ruined!'

She swung her handbag.
Blackbones dodged. He wasn't
used to fighting hopping
mad headteachers.

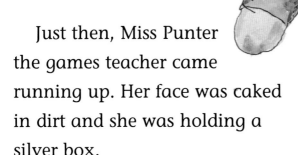

Just then, Miss Punter
the games teacher came
running up. Her face was caked
in dirt and she was holding a
silver box.

'Miss Lupin! Look, I found it!
The buried treasure!' she cried.

'But there wasn't any...' Yasmin
started to say. Tara tried to shut her up.

Miss Punter opened the silver box.
Everyone gasped. Inside were sparkling
jewels and necklaces.

'The treasure map led me straight to
them,' said Miss Punter. 'Just as it said,
X marked the spot.'

Miss Lupin read the name inside the silver box. 'Great Aunt Amelia! These are her jewels! I always knew she'd hidden them somewhere.'

She turned to Captain Blackbones.

'You clever, clever man. But how did you know where they were?'

For a moment Blackbones was lost for words. Then he gave Miss Lupin a wink. 'I felt it in me bones,' he said.

The school was saved. The money from the jewels paid for all the repairs. Miss Lupin had the roof mended. Miss Punter got a new games field.

And as for Blackbones, the pirate teacher, Miss Lupin gave him a new job teaching the children to sail.

This week he took all of Class 4 out in a boat called Salty Sal. They were last seen heading out to sea with the skull and crossbones flying from the mast.

Blackbones was at the wheel, the sea breeze in his hair and a treasure map in his hand. Who knows when they will be back?

About the author

I write for children because
I like making up stories. Some
of my stories are in books
while some have been on
radio or television.

I live in Nottingham with
my wife and three children.
Sometimes we all make up
stories together at bath time.

The idea for this story came from
thinking about pirates. What do they
do when they give up being pirates
I wondered – what if a pirate got a job
as a teacher? Blackbones was born!